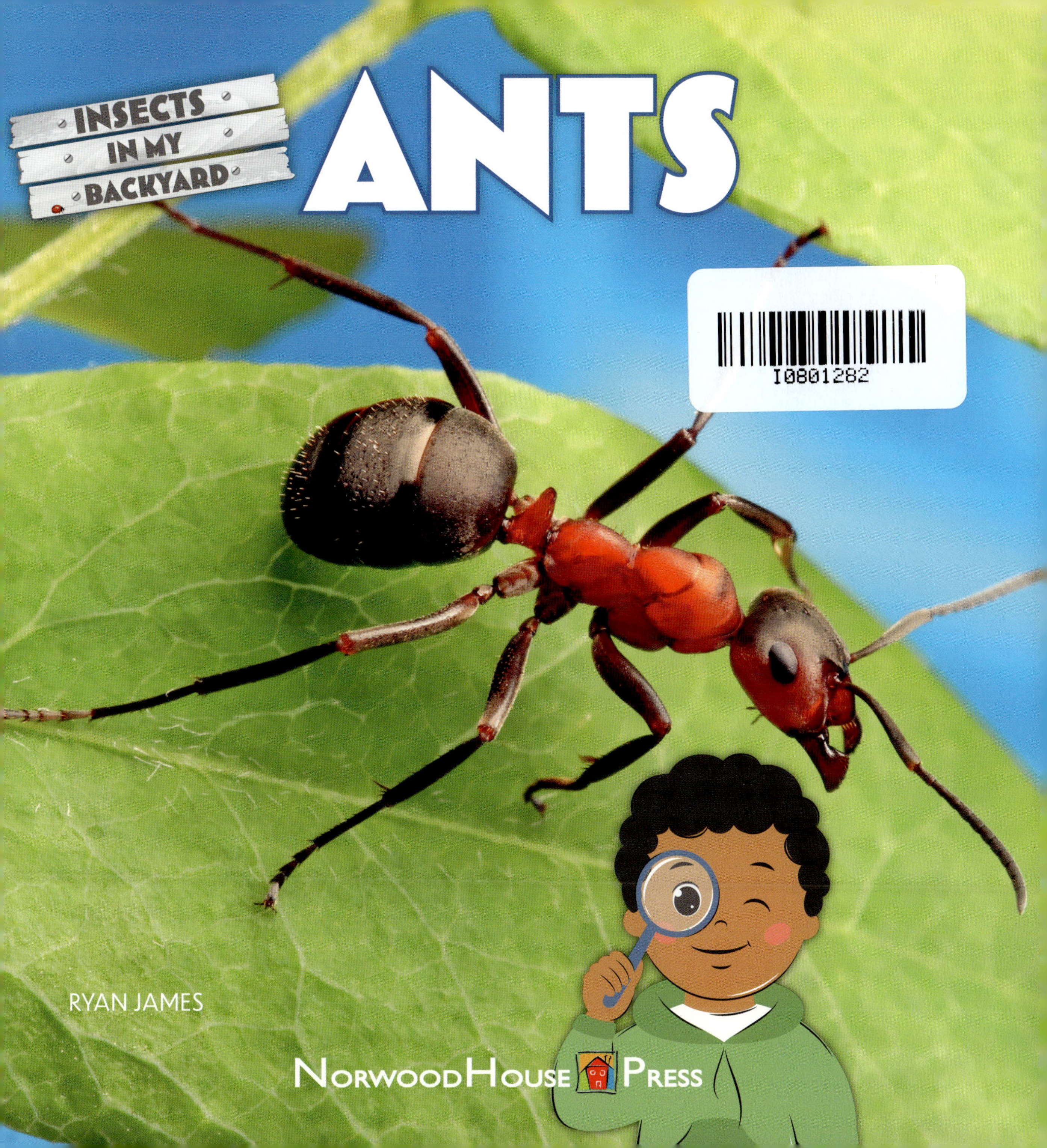

Insects in My Backyard

ANTS

Ryan James

Norwood House Press

Library of Congress Cataloging-in-Publication Data

Names: James, Ryan.
Title: Ants / Ryan James.
Description: Buffalo, NY : Norwood House Press, 2025. | Series: Insects in my backyard | Includes glossary and index.
Identifiers: ISBN 9781684502417 (pbk.) | ISBN 9781684502424 (library bound) | ISBN 9781684502431 (ebook)
Subjects: LCSH: Ants--Juvenile literature. | Ants--Behavior--Juvenile literature. | Ant communities--Juvenile literature.
Classification: LCC QL568.F7 J359 2025 | DDC 595.79'6--dc23

Published in 2025 by
Norwood House Press
2544 Clinton Street
Buffalo, NY 14224

Designer: Ocean Books
Editor: Kim Thompson

Photo credits: Cover, p. 1 Achkin/Shutterstock.com; p. 5 Frank60/Shutterstock.com; p. 6 Jirasak Chuangsen/Shutterstock.com; p. 8 ArtLovePhoto/Shutterstock.com; p. 10 czjonyyy/Shutterstock.com; p. 11 Cherdchai Chaivimol/Shutterstock.com; p. 12 Dmitry Dolhikn/Shutterstock.com; p. 13 Jeremy Christensen; p. 15 Mikolaj Michalak/Shutterstock.com; p. 16 Kiran Nagare/Shutterstock.com; p. 17 KPL/Shutterstock.com; p. 18 BlueSnap; p. 19 chalyaphum soktia/Shutterstock.com; p. 21 Charles Mortensen/Shutterstock.com

Printed in the United States of America

CPSIA compliance information: Batch #CW25NHP: For further information contact Norwood House Press at 1-800-237-9932.

TABLE OF CONTENTS

WHAT IS AN ANT?

Ants are busy **insects** that you might find in your backyard. They live and work together.

BODY PARTS

Ants have three body sections. The head is in front. Here, ants have **antennae** that help them smell and feel. They have strong jaws that help them carry food and defend themselves.

The thorax is the middle section of an ant's body. Six legs are attached here. Ants use their legs to run and climb.

The abdomen is the back section of an ant's body. This part stores food. In some ants, a stinger is found here.

TYPES OF ANTS

In an ant **colony**, different types of ants have different jobs. Most ants are worker ants. They find food, take care of the young, and build the nest.

Soldier ants are bigger and stronger than worker ants. They protect the colony from **predators**.

The queen is the largest ant in the colony. She lays all the eggs to keep the colony growing.

Drone ants are male. They stay in the colony only for a short time. They are the fathers of young ants.

ANT BEHAVIOR

Ants work together to find food. They leave a **scent** trail so that other ants in the colony can find it.

Ants work together to build a nest. They use their strong jaws. They make tunnels and **chambers**.

Ants work together to protect the colony from **threats**. Soldier ants stand guard. They fight predators, including other insects.

WHY ARE ANTS IMPORTANT?

Ants help make the soil healthy by digging tunnels. This lets air and water reach plant roots.

Ants eat **pests** like termites and caterpillars. This helps protect plants and farm crops.

Ants are food for animals like birds and lizards. They are an important part of the food chain.

GLOSSARY

antennae (an-TEN-ee): slender, movable, segmented organs on the heads of insects that are used to sense the environment; feelers

chambers (CHAYM-burz): rooms, especially rooms used for sleeping

colony (KAH-luh-nee): a large group of animals that live together

insects (IN-sekts): small animals that have hard outer skeletons instead of backbones and that have three pairs of legs, one or two pairs of wings, and three body sections

pests (pests): insects or other animals that damage farm crops, that interfere dangerously with human activities, or that annoy people

predators (PRED-uh-turz): animals that live by hunting other animals for food

scent (sent): a distinctive smell, especially a smell that is left behind for others to find or follow

threats (threts): dangers

THINKING QUESTIONS

1. Name an ant's three body sections.
2. Why is the queen ant important?
3. How do ants help others find food?
4. Why are soldier ants bigger than worker ants?
5. Why are ants important?

INDEX

ABOUT THE AUTHOR

Ryan James lives in the western part of North Carolina with his rescue dog Bailey. As a child, he would search for creepy crawlies as he hiked through the forest near his house. When he's not on the hiking or biking trail, he is cheering on his favorite baseball and football teams.